Inventions and Discoveries

Warfare

WORLD BOOK

a Scott Fetzer company

Chicago

www.worldbookonline.com

World Book, Inc.
233 N. Michigan Avenue
Chicago, IL 60601
U.S.A.

For information about other World Book publications, visit our Web site at **http://www.worldbookonline.com** or call **1-800-WORLDBK (967-5325)**.

For information about sales to schools and libraries, call **1-800-975-3250 (United States),** or **1-800-837-5365 (Canada)**.

Editorial:

Editor in Chief: Paul A. Kobasa
Project Manager: Cassie Mayer
Editor: Jake Bumgardner
Writer: Rebecca McEwen
Researcher: Cheryl Graham
Content Development: Odyssey Books
**Manager, Contracts & Compliance
  (Rights & Permissions):** Loranne K. Shields
Indexer: David Pofelski

Graphics and Design:

Associate Director: Sandra M. Dyrlund
Manager: Tom Evans
**Coordinator, Design Development
  and Production:** Brenda B. Tropinski
Senior Designer: Isaiah W. Sheppard, Jr.
Senior Cartographer: John Rejba

Pre-Press and Manufacturing:

Director: Carma Fazio
Manufacturing Manager: Steven K. Hueppchen
Production/Technology Manager: Anne Fritzinger

Library of Congress Cataloging-in-Publication Data

Warfare.
    p. cm. – (Inventions and Discoveries)
  Includes index.
  Summary: "An exploration of the transformative impact of inventions and discoveries in warfare. Features include fact boxes, sidebars, biographies, timeline, glossary, list of recommended reading and Web sites, and index."–Provided by publisher.
  ISBN: 978-0-7166-0388-7
  1. Military art and science--History--Juvenile literature. 2. Military weapons--History--Juvenile literature. I. World Book, Inc.
U106.W325 2009
355.02--dc22
                    2008042946

Picture Acknowledgments:
Front Cover: © Duby Tal, Albatross/Israel Images/Alamy Images.
Back Cover: © The British Library/HIP/The Image Works.

© Peter Connolly, akg-images 8; © nagelestock/Alamy Images 12; © Eileen Tweedy, The Art Archive 19; Werner Forman, Art Resource 11; HIP/Art Resource 30; Erich Lessing, Art Resource 4, 10, 20; Bridgeman Art Library 31; Detail of a Corinthian vase showing a hoplite battle (c. 600 BC), terracotta; Louvre, Paris, France (Peter Willi, Bridgeman Art Library) 7; © Hulton-Deutsch Collection/Corbis 28; © Baldwin and Kathryn Ward, Corbis 37; © Hulton Archive/Getty Images 21; © Imagno/Getty Images 39; © Boyer/Roger-Viollet/Getty Images 23, © Lee Boltin, Time Life Pictures/Getty Images 24; © Alfred Eisenstaedt, Time Life Pictures/Getty Images 41; © Dick Swanson, Time Life Pictures/Getty Images 29; © Topical Press Agency/Getty Images 32; Granger Collection 14, 19, 25, 34, 36, 38; © The British Library/HIP/The Image Works 7, 12; © Stapleton/HIP/The Image Works 8; © Roger-Viollet/The Image Works 29; © Science Museum/SSPL/The Image Works 26; Mary Evans Picture Library 6, 9, 18, 25; The First Muster by Don Troiana (The National Guard) 22; North Wind Picture Archives 15; © SuperStock 5; U.S. Air Force 35, 39, 40; U.S. Navy 5, 15, 23, 27, 33, 42, 43.

All maps and illustrations are the exclusive property of World Book, Inc.

Inventions and Discoveries
Set ISBN: 978-0-7166-0380-1
Printed in China
1 2 3 4 5 13 12 11 10 09

▶ Table of Contents

There is a glossary of terms on pages 45-46. Terms defined in the glossary are in type **that looks like this** on their first appearance on any spread (two facing pages).

▶ Introduction

This stone relief of Egyptian warriors dates from 1300 B.C.

What is an invention?

An invention is a new device, new product, or new way of doing something. Inventions change the way people live. Before the car was invented, some people rode horses to travel long distances. Before the light bulb was invented, people used candles and similar sources of light to see at night. Almost two million years ago, the creation of the spear and the bow and arrow helped people hunt better. Today, inventions continue to change the way people live.

What is warfare?

Warfare describes wars or armed conflicts between groups of people.

Throughout history, people have invented weapons to protect themselves against others. Prehistoric people competed with wild animals for food and territory. Weapons for hunting were among people's earliest tools. People also created weapons for warfare.

In prehistoric times, populations were **nomadic,** small, and spread out, so fighting was rare. When it did happen, people were quick to turn their stone axes, spears, and arrows on each other. As people began farming and forming **civilizations,** the number of people on Earth grew. Territories became more clearly marked and the resources more valuable. People built towns and then cities in locations with plenty of food and water. They developed new tools and technology. On the outside of these civilizations were other groups that wanted to take over these valuable locations and claim the best resources for themselves.

Wars began as fights between families and clans. Later, tribes fought against other tribes to take or protect

Thutmose III

Thutmose (*thoot MOH suh*) III was one of the greatest kings of ancient Egypt. He ruled Egypt from 1479-1425 B.C. Thutmose expanded the Egyptian empire with a succession of 17 wars fought against neighboring people, capturing no less than 350 cities during his reign. He is considered the greatest of the warrior pharaohs (kings) and is credited with making Egypt the dominant superpower of its time. The Battle of Megiddo (1479 B.C.) is the first great battle recorded in detail. Thutmose III and his 10,000 soldiers defeated an army of Canaanites, the ancient people of modern Israel, Palestine, and Lebanon.

possessions (belongings) and power. Over the centuries, war took on an entirely new meaning as cities and governments grew larger and more powerful. Fighting became a profession, and soldiers began fighting wars in distant lands with increasingly dangerous weapons.

Wars today have many causes. Some wars are fought over land, food, and resources, such as oil, a valuable fuel. Others result from a struggle for power. Wars are also fought over the difference of ideas—like religion or politics.

There are many types of war. Civil wars are fought between people of the same country. People fight revolu-tionary wars to overthrow the government of their country. **Cold wars** are fought with language, using power and **diplomacy,** rather than force of arms.

American soldiers patrol in Iraq in 2005.

Early Weapons

More than two million years ago, people created the first spears. These spears were long wooden shafts with a sharpened point. Some ancient people attached a sharpened stone or metal head to the end of their spears. A spear extended the reach of a hunter or warrior beyond arm's length, making it easier to avoid an animal's claws and teeth—or an enemy's knife. Though the spear is an effective weapon, one must still get fairly close to the target to use it.

Prehistoric people also created lighter throwing spears called **javelins** (*JAV uh lihns*). However, these spears were hard to throw accurately and rarely resulted in a kill. When used for hunting, a javelin was likely to bounce off an animal's tough hide.

Over time, the spear became smaller and was used as a projectile—that is, something hurled through the air, like an arrow launched from a tightly strung bow. The bow and arrow let the hunter or warrior stay farther from danger while providing a powerful killing force.

As early as 5000 B.C., ancient Egyptian **archers** used bows and arrows in hunting and in war. Archery is the art of shooting a bow and arrow. A well-trained archer has an advantage over a person fighting with a spear. The first spearheads and arrowheads were made of soft stone, such as flint or obsidian.

In the 400's B.C., many Persian soldiers were armed with spears and bows and arrows.

With the beginning of metal-working, weapons became more powerful. Copper and, later, iron heads were made, making them both stronger and sharper. Bows also improved, gaining strength by the addition of bone and bark layers on the wood. This allowed the archer to bend the bow farther back, causing the arrow to travel farther when the bow was released.

During the **Middle Ages** (A.D. 400's-1400's), people developed the powerful **crossbow.** The crossbow is a mechanical bow that launches an arrow with great speed. To load the crossbow, the archer draws the bowstring back to a catch. To fire the crossbow, the archer pulls a trigger to release the arrow, which flies with so much force that it can pierce protective **armor** from 1,000 feet (about 305 meters) away.

Ancient Greek soldiers were armed with spears and wore protective helmets, shields, and leg armor.

During the Middle Ages, soldiers used the crossbow and the bow and arrow to attack walled towns.

Cavalry

The Battle of Kadesh in 1275 B.C. was the biggest chariot battle ever fought. As many as 5,000 Egyptian and Hittite chariots met in combat.

For thousands of years, nothing was more effective on the battlefield than **cavalry**—that is, a unit of soldiers on horseback. The quickness and strength of horses allowed mounted warriors to strike at the enemy while making it difficult

Alexander the Great used cavalry to defeat the Persians at the Battle of the Granicus in 334 B.C.

for the enemy to strike back.

The **chariot,** a battle cart pulled by two or more horses, became a common sight on the battlefield by about 3000 B.C. Chariots gave armies greater mobility. Their two-man crews could fight on the run, with one person driving while the other—usually an **archer**—fought.

As early as 1500 B.C., Hittites, ancient people who lived in what is now Turkey, and Assyrians and Babylonians, who lived in present-day Iraq, were using cavalry to ride into battle.

During the 300's B.C., the armies of Alexander the Great of Macedonia, a country in southern Europe, made deadly use of mounted warriors. They conquered much of the known world at the time. His cavalry carried heavy lances (long spears),

javelins, and swords. It operated as units designed to strike quickly and strongly before the enemy could organize a defense.

Cavalry was important for communication on the battlefield, since horses were the fastest way to travel between two places. Cavalry also gathered information about the enemy. Mounted soldiers could ride quickly around or through enemy lines to determine troop strength and position.

Between the A.D. 600's and 700's, **Muslim** armies used cavalry to their advantage, expanding their empires all the way from present-day Spain to central Asia. Muslim slave soldiers were specially trained in horsemanship and combat, as well as in honor, courage, and generosity. These are similar to the virtues of chivalry, the code adopted by various knights (mounted warriors) of the **Middle Ages** (A.D. 400's-1400's).

Before the development and improvement of saddles, stirrups, and spurs, fighting on horseback was quite difficult. Soldiers rode their horses into battle, but then they had to dismount to engage in combat.

Cavalry remained an important form of warfare until the end of World War I (1914-1918). After the development of advanced weapons

and vehicles, horse warfare disappeared. Cavalry units began using jeeps, **tanks,** and helicopters to do much the same work that was once performed on horseback.

French cavalry charge the enemy during the 1807 Battle of Friedland.

The Sword

Around 3500 B.C., people began making bronze by melting copper with the chemical element arsenic. Bronze is a hard alloy (metal mixture) that can be hammered or beaten into tools and weapons. As bronze metalworking improved, the blades on knives got longer, creating the sword. The blade of a sword has either one or two cutting edges. In battle, soldiers used these sharp bronze swords to stab at their enemies.

By 1000 B.C., most swords were made of iron, a metal that is harder than bronze and better suited for swordmaking. Most early iron swords were only 18 to 24 inches (46 to 61 centimeters) long.

By about 300 B.C., people had learned to mix iron with the chemical element **carbon** to create steel. Steel makes a much stronger blade than iron. People also made these blades larger and longer than earlier swords.

Eventually, long swords became popular, such as the massive claymore carried by Scottish warriors in the A.D. 1500's. Claymores are very heavy, broad-bladed steel swords nearly 5 feet (more than 1.5 meters) long. This great size was typical of two-handed swords, which were so large and heavy that people had to be very strong to carry and swing them in battle.

Some swords, such as the Persian *scimitar* (*SIHM uh tuhr*), had sharp, curved blades, and were so light that people could hold them in one hand. Many smaller swords, such as the rapier (*RAY pee uhr*), were made for personal self-defense rather than for military use.

Samurai (*SAM u ry*) were Japanese

These swords are all from the late Bronze Age, between 1250 and 850 B.C.

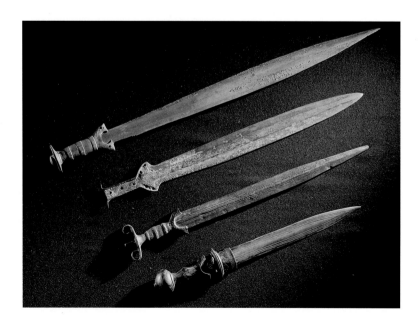

More than 300,000 warriors clashed at the Siege of Osaka Castle in 1615, the last great samurai battle.

warriors of the **Middle Ages** (A.D. 400's-1400's) trained in the art of the sword. The blades of samurai swords were made by heating and hammering up to 10,000 thin layers of steel together. The piece was then heated, folded, and hammered flat many times, until the swordmaker was satisfied. This method eliminated any tiny air pockets that would cause the blade to chip or crack, and made the sword amazingly strong. A sword was the samurai's most prized possession. Samurais believed their soul lived within the carefully crafted metal.

Use of the sword declined with the invention of **gunpowder** and the firearms that followed. However, many military officers continued to carry swords into battle right up through World War I (1914-1918). Today, some military and government officials carry swords as symbols of authority and wealth.

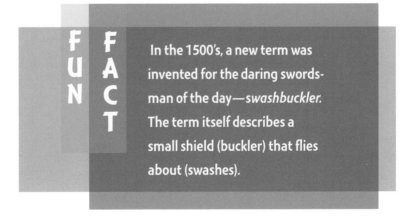

FUN FACT In the 1500's, a new term was invented for the daring swords-man of the day—*swashbuckler.* The term itself describes a small shield (buckler) that flies about (swashes).

Forts and Castles

The Alcázar of Segovia, Spain, was built in the A.D. 1100's on the site of an ancient Roman fort.

Soldiers fire guns at one another during a castle siege in the late 1400's.

For protection, people built some of the first towns on mountains and atop hills. Height is an advantage for the defender. From higher up, people can see a threat coming from far away. Also, an enemy army must fight its way uphill, while the people defending themselves can rain down weapons upon the enemy from above.

Over time, people improved ways to protect themselves. They added walls around the town, which lay on top of a hill. Protective walls can stop attackers in their tracks. The towns-

people could stay safely within the walls in times of emergency. From the windows and the tops of walls, they could shoot arrows and throw boulders (giant rocks), spears, flaming logs, and boiling oil. The enemy, who had already climbed the hill, now had to climb the wall or break through it under constant fire from above.

Eventually, these walls were connected and fortified (strengthened for defense), creating the first forts.

Mud and brick walls gave way to large wooden structures as people tried to make their towns even safer.

Around the late A.D. 900's, European rulers began building castles. At first, these castles were made of earth and wood. But in the 1100's, Europeans began building castles out of stone, which was strong and fireproof. Round towers—which are structurally stronger than square ones—stood at the corners. These towers gave people still more height from which to see. Because people had to stay inside to keep safe, many castles had access to underground streams or canals. Food from the surrounding farms was stored within the castle.

Castle walls had narrow windows. This allowed people inside the castle to shoot arrows at attackers, while only the most accurate of shots by the enemy might reach them. Castles also had holes in the ceilings over gateways and passages. If the enemy somehow got through the outer walls, still more weapons could be fired or dropped through the holes right onto the enemy.

Modern warfare has largely made the castle a thing of the past. How-

Castles had many different features. A moat (deep ditch filled with water) surrounded the outside of the castle, preventing the enemy from reaching it, since soldiers in heavy **armor** could not swim. To get across the moat, one would have to cross the **drawbridge**. The drawbridge would be drawn (pulled up) during an attack. Inside the castle was a blockhouse—a heavily protected place of last resort with thick walls. Castles also commonly had a church or chapel inside.

ever, many of these fortified buildings still stand, proof of the strength and toughness for which they were intended.

► The Catapult

Ancient Romans used catapults to knock down enemies and walls.

After defensive walls and castles were built, attackers came up with ways to knock them down—or to at least get inside them. Wooden walls and **fortresses** (large forts) could be brought down with fire. But stone forts had to be climbed or knocked down.

The **catapult** is an ancient, deadly, and effective weapon that was used to do battle at fortresses. Some catapults work like giant sling-shots. Others work like giant **crossbows.** Either way, they hurl giant objects far and fast using a system of twisted ropes, swinging beams, and weights.

Catapults were the earliest forms of **artillery**—that is, large machines used to fire objects. In 399 B.C., Greek soldiers first used catapults to hurl spears, stones, and other large objects against enemy forces and structures. By A.D. 100, ancient **Roman** armies had many types of catapults, including one that was mounted onto carriages. The carriages could then be moved around the battlefield and used where and when they were needed.

Within the cities, defending soldiers used their own catapults to launch weapons at invaders. They often used the same objects that had just been thrown at them. Defenders also launched less savory things at their opponents, such as **sewage,** garbage, and even dead bodies.

Catapults became even more dangerous when soldiers started using them to shoot burning or explosive materials at enemy forces. Soldiers soaked giant stones or bundles of wood in oil or sulfur and then loaded them into the spring trap of the catapult. They ignited the objects and then launched them through the air, spreading burning fuel wherever the object landed. Hurling fire through the air could cause massive destruction. It was also terrifying to enemy soldiers.

The invention of **gunpowder** made explosive force much stronger and more compact. **Cannons,** which use ignited gunpowder to hurl objects, largely replaced catapults. (See Cannons, pages 24-25.) However, catapults still had some uses. During World War I (1914-1918), soldiers

The catapult was first used in 399 B.C. by Greek soldiers.

used catapults to launch hand **grenades** farther than they could throw them. Today, modern **navies** (armed forces at sea) use catapults to launch airplanes off the short decks of **aircraft carriers.**

A sailor prepares a steam catapult (left) to help launch a fighter jet (right) from the deck of an aircraft carrier.

German
A.D. 1500's

Greek
c. 450 B.C.

European
A.D. 1600's

Roman
c. A.D. 100

The evolution of armor through the ages mirrored the evolution of weaponry.

Body **armor** has been around since ancient times. Prehistoric people wore thick animal skins to soften the blows of clubs and to fend off the sharp points of spears and arrows. Some ancient people wore thick strips of leather strengthened with bronze. Ancient Greeks and **Romans** wore armor made of bronze or steel.

By the **Middle Ages** (A.D. 400's-1400's), armor had become effective, but it was very heavy. Soldiers began wearing entire suits of chain mail—tiny metal rings that linked together and overlapped. Because it was not all one sheet of metal, chain mail was flexible, allowing a soldier to move more easily despite the weight. Soldiers also wore helmets that covered and protected as much of the head and face as possible, sometimes with mere slits through which to see.

Chain mail is strong enough to protect soldiers from most arrows, lances (long spears), and swords. However, **crossbows** and longbows fired arrows with enough force to pierce chain mail. An axe or a mace (a club with a metal head) could crush chain mail, as well as the soft human body beneath it. Large plates of steel began to be worn over chain mail, covering the soldier from head to foot—but weighing him down. A suit of armor could weigh as much as 80 pounds (36 kilograms).

Suits of armor were heavy, uncomfortable, and hot. Soldiers had difficulty walking, running, or moving at all while wearing armor. It became necessary to ride horses for mobility, so the horses had to be especially big and strong and were also covered with armor. It was very expensive to pay for the horse, the weapons, and all that armor—the same price as a small farm!

Firearms changed the nature of armor. To be thick and heavy enough to stop a bullet, armor would become too heavy to wear. Before long, people wore only helmets and breastplates into battle. By the end of World War I (1914-1918), soldiers wore protective helmets but rarely any other armor.

Today, modern technology has created armor that can withstand many kinds of weapons and is light enough to wear. Soldiers and police wear "flak jackets," which are a type of bulletproof vest that will stop most small arms and **shrapnel.**

A CLOSER LOOK

Today, some bulletproof vests have ceramic plates or tiles stitched into the fabric. When a bullet hits the hardness of the tile, it slows down enough that it will not travel all the way through the vest, although it will smash the tile. In a textile (woven fabric) bulletproof vest, many layers of a heavy nylon cloth are stitched together like a quilt. When a bullet is fired at one of these vests, it flattens out as it hits the outer layers of nylon, but it does not pass all the way through the vest.

Gladiators dueled in the arenas of ancient Rome. Some wore special helmets and carried protective shields.

Gunpowder

Gunpowder is an explosive material used to propel such objects as bullets and **rockets.** Early gunpowder was made from a mixture of saltpeter (a salty, white mineral), charcoal, and the chemical element sulfur.

The first people to learn about gunpowder's fiery nature were the Chinese. At first, they drank gunpowder like a tea, believing that it benefited their health. After they realized their mistake, they started using gunpowder to make explosions. By A.D. 800, fireworks displays were lighting up the skies in China. A century later, the Chinese were using it in warfare to ignite arrows and to make rockets, bombs, and flamethrowers.

Gunpowder technology spread slowly through the Arab world to Europe. By the early 1300's, people used gunpowder to shoot heavy iron balls out of **cannons.** Burning gunpowder shot the cannonball at such a high speed that its force could break through castle walls. Before long, cannonballs themselves were stuffed with gunpowder, exploding when they hit their target.

Traditional gunpowder produces thick clouds of smoke, making its use obvious to anyone around. A hidden **rifle** or cannon is not hidden after firing because the smoke gives the location away. Also, when many rifles and cannons fired on the battlefield, the resulting smoke made it difficult to see. Many battles have been won and lost because of the confusion caused by dense clouds of smoke on the battlefield.

Ancient Chinese emperors sometimes used gunpowder to scare off their enemies.

Smokeless gunpowder appeared in the 1800's. It was produced from guncotton, an explosive made from cotton soaked in nitric acid. Smokeless powder produced much more gas and much less smoke than traditional gunpowder, making it ideal for use in firearms. However, it was much more dangerous to produce and use.

Today, acidic compounds have replaced gunpowder in many larger weapons, such as bombs and cannons. Most of these compounds are called high explosives because they burn at a much higher rate than gunpowder, making them much more powerful. Dynamite and TNT are the most famous of these chemical explosives.

Skilled tradesmen made gunpowder in Europe during the 1700's.

On July 14, 1789, rebels stormed the Bastille Prison in Paris to steal 30,000 pounds (13,600 kilograms) of gunpowder.

▶ Guns

An early type of gun was a small, handheld **cannon** (or "hand cannon") that may have appeared as early as the A.D. 1200's in China. To operate the weapon, a person packed **gunpowder** into a bamboo tube, placed a small stone into the other end, and ignited the gunpowder. The stone would shoot out of the tube at great speed.

The earliest record of a hand cannon used in battle dates to 1269. The hand cannon was difficult to use because it took three hands to work—two to hold the weapon steady and one to ignite the powder.

Firing a gun became much easier in the late 1300's, when the **matchlock** was invented. This mechanical device held a slow-burning match in a clamp near the end of the gun **barrel** (the metal tube). When a soldier pulled the trigger on the bottom of the gun, the match lowered, igniting the gunpowder in the barrel. Soldiers could fire the matchlock gun more quickly and accurately than the hand cannon because they could aim steadily without having to check that they were properly lighting the gun.

Though the invention of the matchlock improved gun design, early guns were still difficult to use during battles. They took a long time to load and were unreliable. Sometimes the gunpowder did not ignite, which

The harquebus could shoot right through heavy armor. At short range, it was loud and deadly.

meant the gun would not fire. Even worse, sometimes the entire gun exploded. In the heat of battle, with swords slashing and arrows flying past, the early gun was not always the best weapon.

The harquebus (*HAHR kwuh buhs*) was an early firearm that developed from the hand cannon. It was the first matchlock gun to load from the muzzle, the opening at the front end of the barrel. The harquebus was not as accurate as the bow and arrow, but it was easier and faster to use and more powerful. The loud *bang* of the harquebus also helped its effectiveness, scaring enemy soldiers and horses alike.

Improvements to the gun led to many new types of firearms that would change how wars were fought. (See Rifles, Repeaters, and Machine Guns, pages 24-25.)

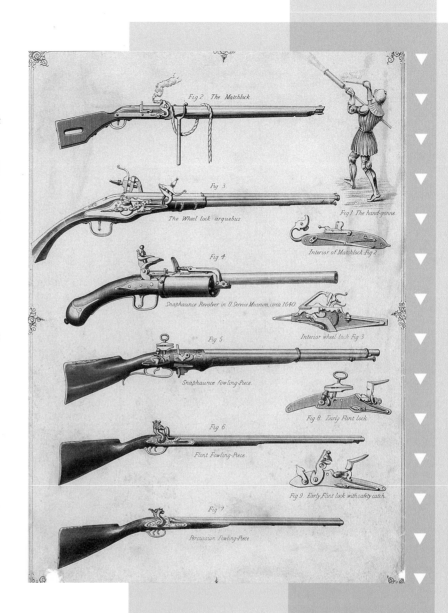

(See Rifles, Repeaters, and Machine Guns, pages 24-25.)

F U N F A C T

When early musketeers heard the order "Give fire," they would press the trigger of their muskets so the match would slide down into the gunpowder and light it. By the early 1700's, this order was shortened to "Fire!"

This engraving from the 1800's shows (top to bottom) a matchlock, a harquebus, an early revolver, and three "fowling pieces" —shotguns for hunting fowl (birds).

▶ Rifles, Repeaters, and Machine Guns

The U.S. National Guard began with the Massachusetts Bay Colony militia in 1637. Here, they train in the use of the musket.

By the A.D. 1300's, the Chinese were using a gun with an elongated muzzle that is now known as the **musket.** The musket was a muzzle-loaded firearm and was a forerunner to the **rifle.** Early muskets were 6 or 7 feet (1.8 to 2.1 meters) long and weighed as much as 40 pounds (18 kilograms). The musket spread through Europe by the 1500's.

At close range (distance), muskets could shoot through **armor.** But muskets were very inaccurate, making it difficult to hit a target more than 100 yards (91 meters) away.

In battle, soldiers had to stand in a line and fire together at the enemy. If they all hid and fired individually, very few people would have been shot.

The first rifles were developed in Europe in the mid-1600's. A rifle is similar to a musket, but it has spiral grooves inside the **barrel** that spin the bullet, causing it to travel in a more controlled path. Rifles were more accurate than any previous firearms, but they were harder to load and more difficult to manufacture. Rifles were not widely used by soldiers until the 1800's, when technology finally allowed for accurate production of large numbers of rifles.

Early weapons like the rifle were single-shot guns that had to be reloaded each time they were fired. The repeating rifle, developed in 1860, could fire several shots without reloading. Repeating rifles use a magazine—that is, a simple **ammunition** chamber that holds several cartridges (cases holding **gunpowder** and a bullet or shot). After a shot is fired, a **lever** throws out the used shell and inserts a new cartridge. Repeaters reduced the amount of time it took to load the gun from 20 seconds at best to less than one second.

In the 1860's, the American inventor Richard Gatling developed an even faster firing gun. The Gatling gun was roughly the size of a **cannon** and had 10 rotating barrels that were turned by a hand crank. The gun could fire 200 shots per minute, unheard-of speed for its day.

An American-born inventor named Hiram Maxim developed one of the first fully automatic machine guns in 1883. The Maxim gun could fire 600 rounds of ammunition per minute. It used strips of ammunition arranged on a belt, which was fed through the machine. The U.S. Army started using Maxim machine guns in 1887. In World War I (1914-1918),

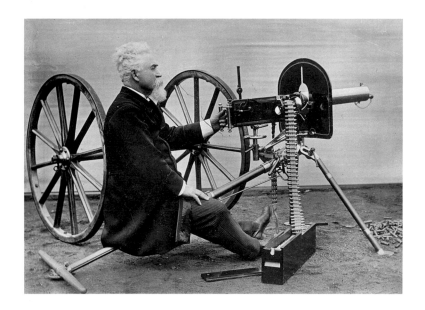

soldiers on both sides were using machine guns on the ground, on board ships, and even in the air, mounted to the earliest airplanes.

Today, machine guns are still used in battle. Modern machine guns can fire anywhere from 400 to 1,600 rounds of ammunition per minute.

Hiram Maxim sits with his machine gun around 1900.

This modern machine gun can fire between 750 and 950 rounds per minute.

Cannons and Other Artillery

By about A.D. 1350, armies developed one of the biggest, most destructive weapons used on the battlefield: the **cannon.** Cannons are powerful, tube-shaped guns that are too large to be carried by hand. They are part of a group of weapons called **artillery,** which includes heavy guns that fire large **ammunition.**

This French engraving from the 1600's shows the powerful potential of field artillery. The gunners use indirect fire to attack a fortified town.

The first cannons were made of bronze or cast iron and were used to knock down the walls of castles. Cannons were also used at sea. They were often placed on large warships and used to punch holes in enemy ships and set them on fire. **Naval** guns fired either cannonballs or chain-shot—two small cannonballs that were attached by a chain. Chain-shot could rip through the masts and sails of a ship, leaving it dead in the water.

Cannons changed quickly in size and appearance. By the 1400's, many armies were using massive cannons on the battlefield. Their size and power continued to grow over the next several hundred years.

To protect themselves from cannons, people inside **fortresses** began arranging their own cannons in batteries (groups) along fortress walls. Battery fire made any approach deadly. To counteract batteries, armies developed field artillery—that is, artillery that can be moved relatively easily to the place where it is needed. In the early

Big Bertha was the name given to a massive German howitzer used during World War I (1914-1918). The barrel on Big Bertha was nearly 17 inches (42 centimeters) across. The gun itself weighed 150 tons (136 metric tons). It was so heavy that it had to be transported in sections on 10 railcars. The gun fired shells weighing 2,600 pounds (1,160 kilograms) that could travel a distance of more than 9 miles (15 kilometers). It took a crew of 285 men to maintain the gun, which could only fire 8 rounds in an hour.

1800's, French general and emperor Napoleon Bonaparte used his mastery of field artillery to conquer most of Europe.

Different types of field artillery were developed for special purposes. The mortar is a short-range weapon that is used to reach nearby targets that are protected by hills or other obstacles. It fires an object nearly straight up into the air, allowing it to clear obstacles. Early mortars were used to drop an explosive on the other side of fortress walls.

The howitzer is a medium-size artillery piece similar to the mortar, though its **barrel** can be two to three times as long. Howitzers are more powerful weapons than mortars and can shoot projectiles farther.

Cannons, mortars, and howitzers were first used against **fortifications,** but they have also been used against soldiers. In World War I (1914-1918), the great majority of soldiers killed in combat died of artillery wounds. Artillery continues to play an important role in modern warfare throughout the world.

A German mortar team prepares to fire their weapon in 1940.

▶ Rockets and Guided Missiles

A **rocket** is an engine that produces more power than any other type of engine. It consists of a tube that is open at one end and filled with a substance that burns very rapidly as fuel. The burning fuel creates expanding gases, which escape from the open end of the tube. This causes the rocket to move rapidly upward or forward.

Congreve rocket launchers were used in the Napoleonic Wars (1803-1815).

Fig.3.

Historians believe that the Chinese developed rockets for fireworks and warfare by the A.D. 1200's. After that, rocket technology did not advance much until the early 1800's, when Colonel William Congreve of the British Army developed rockets that could carry explosives.

Congreve's rockets weighed about 32 pounds (15 kilograms) each. They could travel 1.75 miles (2.7 kilometers). The British used these rockets against American soldiers during the War of 1812 (1812-1815). Austria, Russia, and several other countries also developed military rockets during the early 1800's.

Over the next 100 years, rockets became more common on the battlefield. During World War II (1939-1945), the Germans developed the first **guided missiles.** Such missiles could be steered toward their target using **radio waves,** compasses and timers, or **radar.**

Germany launched these guided missiles at enemy cities during World War II. It called the missiles the V-1 and V-2. The V-1 "flying bomb" was 25 feet (7.6 meters) long and carried a ton (0.9 metric ton) of explosives. It was powered by a jet engine and flew at a speed of 360 miles (580 kilometers) per hour. The V-2 missile was rocket-powered and flew at a speed of 3,300 miles (5,311 kilometers) per hour—faster than the speed of sound. These rockets could fly a distance of up to 200 miles (320 kilometers). During the war, more than 7,000 people were killed in rocket attacks across England, Belgium, and France.

After World War II, the United States and the country then known as the Soviet Union continued to develop advanced missile technology. They built rockets for space exploration, but they also built many missiles as weaponry.

Modern missiles have different methods of reaching their targets and can even hit moving targets. Some have video cameras built into them. A person can direct them by remote control, watching the flight on a monitor. Others have computer guidance systems that direct the missile to its target.

Today, some missiles can travel around the world. Others are specially designed to shoot down other missiles. Missile systems are the pri-

mary weapons for many ships, warplanes, and helicopters. They are also used by soldiers on the ground trying to shoot aircraft out of the sky.

A Tomahawk cruise missile launches from an American warship in 2003.

▶ Chemical Warfare

German storm troopers emerge from a cloud of poisonous gas during a battle in World War I.

Since ancient times, people have used forms of **chemical warfare** to fight enemies. Chemical warfare is the use of a poisonous substance with the intention to harm or kill others.

Chemical warfare began when people found things in nature that could be used to harm others. By 10,000 B.C., people used arrows poisoned with snake or scorpion venom. By 400 B.C., the Chinese were clearing enemy tunnels with smoke by burning poisonous plants and chemicals. At around the same time, people in ancient Greece used burning pitch (a sticky substance) and sulfur (an odorous gas) to create poisonous fumes in battle.

Ancient people also used **germs** and disease as a type of weapon. Soldiers sometimes threw bodies of people who died from plague over the walls of cities or into water wells. Hundreds of years later, during the French and Indian wars (1689-1763), blankets used by smallpox victims were given to Native Americans in the hope that they would become infected with the deadly disease.

The first use of modern chemical weapons occurred during World War I (1914-1918). The French army sprayed German soldiers with tear gas, which irritates the eyes and temporarily blinds them with tears. The Germans responded with a sneezing gas and then, in 1915, poi-

A CLOSER LOOK

In the 1960's and early 1970's, the United States armed forces sprayed a weedkiller called Agent Orange over jungles and farms in South Vietnam and Laos. Agent Orange was used to cause the leaves to fall off trees and shrubs and to kill crop plants. The spraying revealed enemy hiding places and destroyed food supplies. Agent Orange is also believed to have caused long-term health effects in people exposed to it. In 1993, the Institute of Medicine, an adviser to the U.S. government, released a study that linked exposure to Agent Orange to three kinds of cancer and two skin diseases.

sonous **chlorine** gas. At first, soldiers simply opened containers of gas and let the wind carry the poisonous cloud over the enemy. Later, **artillery** shells carrying poison gas were fired into and behind enemy lines. The use of gas evolved and escalated on both sides throughout the war.

In 1925, many world leaders signed an agreement forbidding the use chemical or biological weapons, but they still manufactured and stored them. They perfected blistering agents, which burn a person's skin, eyes, windpipe, and lungs. They developed suffocating nerve agents, which are the deadliest chemical weapons of all. If a single drop of certain nerve agents lands on exposed skin or is inhaled, it shuts down breathing and stops the heart.

By 2000, 129 nations had signed an agreement outlawing the production and use of chemical weapons.

U.S. Marines wear gas masks in Saudi Arabia during the Persian Gulf War of 1991.

Early Warships

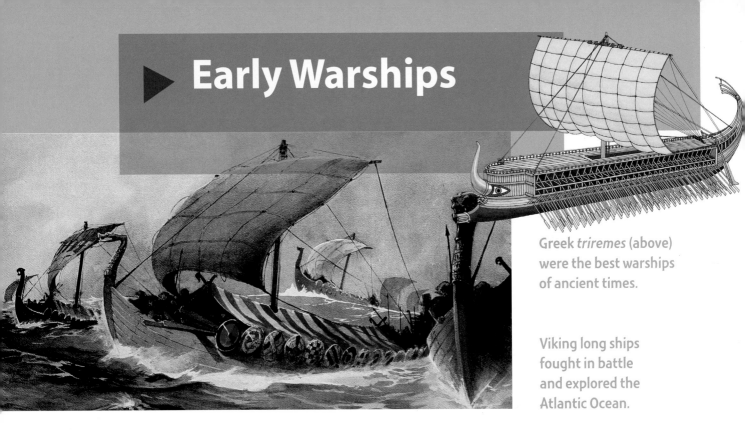

Greek *triremes* (above) were the best warships of ancient times.

Viking long ships fought in battle and explored the Atlantic Ocean.

Since ancient times, ships have been used for war at sea. The ancient **Roman** and Greek **navies** built galleys—long, narrow, wooden ships powered by sails or rows of oarsmen. Most galleys had sharp bronze rams on the bow (front) of the ship, which were used to pierce through enemy ships and sink them. But early warships served mostly as vessels for transporting troops, who would board enemy ships to do battle.

In the A.D. 700's, Vikings (a group of pirates and warriors in northern Europe) used similar ships as they explored the oceans and raided foreign lands. The Viking long ships were strong enough to face the large waves in the open ocean, yet they only weighed about half as much as the Greek and Roman galleys. For about 300 years, long ships carried Vikings great distances, allowing them to control the Arctic and northern Atlantic oceans.

The invention of **gunpowder** changed warfare at sea as much as it did on land. By the 1500's, navies were building warships that resembled floating gun platforms. During this time, the Spanish navy constructed massive galleons—heavy sailing ships suited to long ocean voyages. In 1588, the Spanish navy sailed north to attack England. For defense, the English navy relied on their own smaller, faster galleons.

These ships were able to out-maneuver the Spanish, and they won the battle.

Spain's defeat proved that sheer size was not the most important thing at sea. In the 1600's and 1700's, many European navies constructed vessels called capital ships, which were easy to maneuver but large enough to carry more than 100 guns.

In 1814, the American artist and inventor Robert Fulton built the first warship that was powered by a **steam engine.** Up until the mid-1800's, navies built ships that were powered with a combination of wind and steam. Navies also started experimenting with guns that could shoot explosive shells. These shells could blow huge holes into the sides of ships.

To protect themselves against the explosive shells, navies built ships covered in sheets of iron. The first battle of steam-powered, ironclad ships occurred in 1862 during the American Civil War (1861-1865).

Throughout the 1900's, improvements to warships continued, creating modern navies that play an important role in warfare today.

English ships meet the galleons of the Spanish Armada off the coast of France in 1588.

▶ Modern Warships

The British *Dreadnought* was the fastest and most heavily armed battleship of its day.

The 1900's brought new types of warships to the seas. In 1906, the British Navy launched *Dreadnought* ("fear nothing"), the first modern **battleship.** A battleship is a huge warship that is more heavily armed than any other type of combat ship.

The British battleship featured revolving **turrets** with large guns that could fire in any direction. The *Dreadnought* set the standard for all battleships that **navies** built from that time on. Ships had to be heavily armed and even more heavily **armored.** They had to be large and fast and have efficient communications systems. Before long,

countries measured their strength by the number of battleships their navies commanded.

The fight went beneath the waves with the development of the **submarine.** The first combat submarine was used by the American colonists during the American Revolution (1775-1783). However, submarines did not become effective instruments of war until the early 1900's. The Germans perfected submarine technology with their U-boats, which sank thousands of ships during World War I (1914-1918). Submarines were also an important part of warfare during World War II (1939-1945).

In the early 1900's, heavy guns on land and at sea were overtaken by the development of armed airplanes. Airplanes carrying bombs and small **cannons** were much more powerful than heavy guns. They could also hit targets that were farther away.

Aerial warfare led to the development of **aircraft carriers,** ships that were like floating runways. These ships launch aircraft to attack and defend in battle. The British developed the first

On December 7, 1941, the Japanese launched a surprise attack on the U.S. naval base at Pearl Harbor on the island of Oahu in Hawaii. Many of America's most powerful ships were destroyed, but it was a hollow Japanese victory. Their main targets—the U.S. Navy's three largest aircraft carriers—were not at the base when it was attacked. Five months later, the Japanese were stopped by the American carrier force at the Battle of the Coral Sea. They were soundly defeated a month later at the Battle of Midway. Both of these immense sea battles were fought entirely by warplanes. Neither group of ships ever saw or fired upon the other.

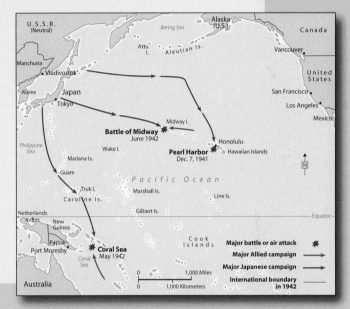

aircraft carrier in 1914. By the end of World War II, aircraft carriers had permanently replaced battleships as the premier fighting ships of the sea.

Today, modern warships continue to serve many important roles. They are used in blockades, where they stop sea traffic, and in convoys, where they protect other ships from submarines. Some warships have been used to support land invasions and to defend against attacking warplanes. Navies continue to develop aircraft carriers. Some are the size of small cities. They allow a country to maintain a naval presence far from its home shores.

The American aircraft carrier *Harry S. Truman* carries more than 5,000 sailors and air crew. It is seen here in 2003 in the Mediterranean Sea.

French tanks parade through the streets of Paris at the end of World War I.

The first half of the 1900's saw many new inventions in warfare. This was mainly due to World War I (1914-1918) and World War II (1939-1945), two of the deadliest and most destructive wars in human history. The **tank** played an important role in both wars. However, it was first developed by the British government to bring an end to World War I.

World War I was a struggle for power involving many countries in Europe. At the beginning of the war, the two sides mainly consisted of the Allies—France, Russia, and the United Kingdom—and the Central Powers, which included Austria-Hungary and Germany. Many more countries joined the war later on, including the United States, which fought on the side of the Allies.

By 1915, both the Allies and Central Powers had dug a system of **trenches**—long, narrow ditches from which soldiers could fire against the enemy. Life in the trenches was miserable. The smell of dead bodies lingered in the air, and rats were a constant problem. On top of these poor living conditions, trench warfare did not advance the war for either side, despite numerous battles and many lives lost.

In order to break the deadlock of trench warfare, the British began a top-secret program to develop new **armored** land vehicles. These massive vehicles, called tanks, weighed nearly 31 tons (28 metric tons). They ran on two continuous treads and reached a maximum speed of less than 4 miles (6 kilometers) per hour.

Each tank needed a crew of eight to operate it and fire its two heavy guns and four machine guns.

Tanks could withstand fire from small arms while using their long bodies and treads to cross deep trenches and shell holes. Tanks, with their firepower, protection, and mobility, served their purpose and played a big part in ending trench warfare and bringing victory to the Allies. During World War II (1939-1945), every country fighting in the war used tanks.

Tanks continue to play an important role in modern warfare. Modern tanks carry **cannons,** machine guns, **grenade** launchers, and even anti-air-craft weapons. They can travel as fast as 50 miles (80 kilometers) per hour on level ground.

Tanks dash through the Egyptian desert in 2001.

A CLOSER LOOK

In the autumn of 1914, the armies of the Allies and Central Powers could advance no further against each other on the **Western Front**. From Switzerland to the English Channel, they each dug a line of trenches, facing each other across a disputed area known as "no man's land." For years, the enemies sat deadlocked in trench warfare. Many millions of men lived in terrible conditions in the trenches, and many of them died there. The trench deadlock was finally broken in 1918, and Germany was defeated.

▶ Airships

Aerial warfare developed mainly during the 1900's, but it had its beginnings much earlier. In ancient China, kites were used to lift men into the air for observation and attack. They also lifted lanterns, long strings, and leaflets to send signals or confuse the enemy.

Balloons were also used in warfare. In 1794, French forces used them to observe enemy troop locations and to direct the movements of French troops. In the American Civil War (1861-1865) and World War I (1914-1918), all armies involved used balloons for observation.

In the 1800's, a new type of flying vehicle, called the **airship,** evolved from balloons. An airship is a type of aircraft that is equipped with an engine and filled with a lighter-than-air gas to raise it and keep it in the air. Early airships had no major internal structures. When filled with air, they would inflate, much like a balloon. However, unlike balloons, airships could be steered, although not too easily at first.

Henri Giffard, a French **engineer,**

Air balloon designs from the 1600's and 1700's looked like ships of the sky.

built and piloted the first powered airship in the 1850's. Giffard's cigar-shaped airship was powered by a **steam engine** and reached an average speed of 5 miles (8 kilometers) per hour. It included a saillike rudder for steering.

Several inventors improved the airship, making it bigger, faster, and easier to steer. A German inventor named Count Ferdinand von Zeppelin designed several new airship models, which came to be known as zeppelins. These were some of the first rigid airships. They had a framework to support the outer shell. One zeppelin model was more than 420 feet (128 meters) long and could reach a top speed of about 17 miles (27 kilometers) per hour.

During World War I (1914-1918), Germany used zeppelins and other airships to gather information about the location of enemy ships and to protect ships against submarine attack. They also used airships to bomb cities, but these raids were not largely successful. Allied countries, including the United Kingdom, the United States, France, and Italy, also used airships during the war for patrolling and defense.

After World War I, airship technology continued to improve. Hydrogen gas, a highly flammable gas that had previously been used to power airships, was replaced with helium gas. In the 1920's and 1930's, the U.S. Navy developed airships that could carry **fighter** airplanes for launch during battle. By World War II (1939-1945),

airplane technology had greatly improved. Fighters and **bombers** largely replaced airship use by the military.

Airships were also used to carry passengers. Airship passenger services reached their height in the 1930's, but a series of disastrous crashes and the increasing popularity and long-range capability of the airplane brought airship passenger services to an end.

The U.S. Navy airship *Macon* carried and launched five small fighter planes. It first launched in 1933 and crashed just two years later.

A CLOSER LOOK

There are three types of airships: (1) nonrigid airships, (2) rigid airships, and (3) semirigid airships. Nonrigid airships have no major internal structures and no outer framework. Gas pressure causes the outer skin to keep its shape. Rigid airships have a rigid framework that supports the outer skin. Semirigid airships often resembled nonrigid ships, except that a support ran along most of the length of the envelope and helped maintain its shape and distribute loads.

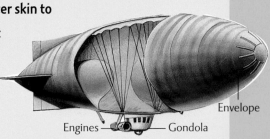

Engines — Gondola

Envelope

Nonrigid airship

Fighters and Bombers

U.S. Army Air Force B-29 bombers drop their deadly weapons during World War II.

At the beginning of World War I (1914-1918), the airplane was still a relatively new invention. Airplanes were somewhat rickety, slow, unreliable, and dangerous contraptions. By the end of the war, warplanes were fast, sturdy, and dependable. Of the many different types of warplanes, **fighters** and **bombers** emerged as the premier weapons of the air. Fighter planes, or fighters, were meant to combat other planes in the sky. Bombers were meant to destroy targets on the ground.

At first, fighters were small, one-man machines that engaged in single combat. Fighter pilots, the knights of the air, became celebrities—if they lived long enough. The average life span of a rookie (inexperienced) fighter pilot on the **Western Front** was between two and three weeks. Most deaths happened in combat, but many airmen were killed in flying accidents.

Bombers are much larger than fighter planes. In World War I, bombers carried as many as four engines, four men, four machine guns, and a load of bombs weighing as much as 4,400 pounds (2,000 kilograms). They could smash rail yards, **ammunition** storehouses, and oil and gasoline tanks. However, they were easy pickings for enemy fighters if they were caught alone. Fighter planes traveled in groups to protect the bombers.

Fighters and bombers played an important role in World War II (1939-1945). The war involved many countries and spread to nearly every part of the world. Countries including the United Kingdom, the United

States, Canada, China, the Soviet Union, and many others fought against Germany, Italy, and Japan. Victory on the ground and at sea almost always depended upon controlling the skies. Nothing was safe from air attack, no matter where or what it was. It wasn't exactly safe in the sky either. More than 500,000 airmen in World War II died.

By the end of World War II, fighters were flying more than 400 miles (644 kilometers) per hour, at altitudes (heights) reaching 40,000 feet. Giant bombers flew more than 5,800 miles (9,300 kilometers) without stopping, carrying 20,000 pounds (91,000 kilograms) of bombs.

Today, fighters and bombers are still an important part of a military's air force. Improved technology and design have advanced the speed and capabilities of fighters and bombers.

Raptor fighter jets use stealth technology, which makes them difficult to see on radar.

Baron Manfred von Richthofen

Baron Manfred von Richthofen (1892–1918), the "Red Baron," was a leading German fighter pilot of World War I. Von Richthofen shot down numerous enemy planes, and once even managed to land his plane after being shot in the head. He commanded a fighter group known as the "Flying Circus" due to their dazzling feats in the air and the flashy colors of their airplanes (von Richthofen's plane was red). He was a superstar in his day, celebrated in newspapers, and even treated to publicity tours while on leave from the front. Short of his 26th birthday, von Richthofen was shot down and killed in France on April 21, 1918.

▶ Nuclear Weapons

A dense mushroom cloud rises over the city of Nagasaki, Japan, in 1945. It was the second and last instance where an atomic weapon was used in warfare.

At the end of World War II (1939-1945), United States **bombers** dropped a new and highly destructive weapon on the cities of Nagasaki and Hiroshima in Japan. The weapon, called the **atomic bomb,** instantly killed nearly 150,000 people and largely destroyed both cities. It was the first and only instance in history where **nuclear weapons** have been used against people.

A nuclear weapon is an explosive device that gets its destructive power from the transformation of matter in **atoms** into energy. An atom is the smallest part of an element—like hydrogen or uranium. It is so small you can't see it. Its nucleus (center) is made up of electrons (negative energy) and protons (positive energy) that hold the atom together like a magnet.

Nuclear reactions occur when the centers of different atoms collide, resulting in the centers breaking apart or joining together. Huge amounts of energy are released by nuclear reactions—enough to make a bomb.

In 1939, the German-born scientist Albert Einstein warned the United States that Germany was trying to develop an atomic bomb. The U.S. government reacted by beginning an atomic program of its own, called the Manhattan Project. As World War II continued to rage, a team of scientists and researchers led by J. Robert Oppenheimer developed the atomic bomb.

The scientists tested the bomb in Alamogordo, New Mexico, on July 16, 1945. The single blast of intense white and then orange light lit up the dark morning like a second sun, forming a giant mushroom cloud 30,000 feet (more than 9 kilometers) above the desert. It was the first detonation of an atomic bomb. The splitting of these atoms led to an explosion equal to 20,000 tons (more than 18,000 metric tons) of dynamite.

Just one month after this test, the United States dropped atomic bombs on Hiroshima and Nagasaki. Japan surrendered about a week later, ending World War II.

Since the end of World War II, many nations have made attempts to prevent the spread of nuclear weapons to countries that do not yet

J. Robert Oppenheimer

J. Robert Oppenheimer (1904–1967) was an American scientist who has often been called "the father of the atomic bomb." Working in a laboratory in Los Alamos, New Mexico, he directed the research that led to the first atomic bomb. Before his work on the Manhattan Project, Oppenheimer was a professor of physics at the University of California. Aside from science, Oppenheimer had the amazing ability to learn languages quickly and completely. He once learned Dutch in just six weeks so he could give a technical talk in the Netherlands.

have them. In 1968, the **United Nations** approved the Treaty on the Non-Proliferation of Nuclear Weapons. The treaty has since been ratified (approved) by nearly all countries. In 1996, the United Nations approved the Comprehensive Nuclear Test Ban Treaty, which would end all testing of nuclear weapons. About three-fourths of the countries that have devices for producing nuclear energy have ratified the treaty.

▶ Recent Inventions in Warfare

Recent advances in warfare technology have helped improve the chances of soldiers' survival at war. Pilots still fly dangerous missions, but they can now fly fewer of them, fly them faster, and fire their weapons from farther away. Observers must still occasionally see the battlefield in person, but they can do most of their work from computers, looking at detailed images of enemy troops and their movements as seen by spy **satellites** in space. Soldiers must still fight battles in the field, but they have better, more accurate and farther-reaching weapons, along with better body **armor** and communication tools.

One recent advancement in warfare technology is the **unmanned aerial vehicle (UAV),** an airplane that can fly missions without a pilot on board. UAV's can be controlled remotely (from a distance), but they can also be programmed to do all the fighting on their own, freeing up people for other jobs. For example, UAV's can read and interpret the landscape,

An unmanned aerial vehicle launches from the deck of a warship in 2006.

A pilot inspects a laser-guided bomb beneath the wing of his aircraft in 2004.

and recognize and fire upon targets. Of course, mechanical error in such a machine could be devastating, so an element of human control remains. A controller might authorize the use of weapons or remove a safety when the UAV encounters an enemy.

UAV's are already used by armies and police around the world, where they can perform reconnaissance (information gathering), firefighting, and bomb detection or demolition (destruction).

Lasers are now used to guide and aim weapons, and there are laser beams that can burn holes in any metal. But most laser technology, like rayguns and plasma **rifles** (rifles that fire intense electric pulses) are still more science fiction than science.

Research is also being done on drugs that may help soldiers during battle. Some of these drugs may help soldiers manage stress and lack of sleep.

Wars themselves have changed and will continue to change. Though conflicts in the past were traditionally fought between entire nations or groups of nations, smaller conflicts dominate the battlefield landscape of today. Smaller conflicts force military leaders and governments to stick to conventional warfare– that is, war without chemical, biological, or **nuclear weapons.**

Important Dates in Warfare

c. 3000 B.C. Mesopotamians built walls around their cities.

c. 1500 B.C. Hittites, Assyrians, and Babylonians started riding horses into battles.

c. 1000 B.C. Europeans began building hill forts.

c. 400's B.C. Sparta used the first-known chemical weapons.

339 B.C. The catapult was invented.

c. A.D. 850 The Chinese discovered gunpowder.

c. 1000's and 1100's European armies modified and improved the structure and performance of bows and arrows, including the crossbow.

c. A.D. 1100 English rulers began building early castles.

1200's Soldiers began wearing armor made from chain mail.

Mid-1300's King Edward III's troops were firing crude cannons on the battlefields in England and Scotland.

Late 1300's The longbow was developed in Europe.

Late 1500's The musket was invented.

1770's The world's first submarine was invented.

1784 The French army conducted intelligence-gathering missions using balloons.

Early 1800's William Congreve of Great Britain designed rockets to carry explosives.

1814 Robert Fulton of the United States built the first steam-powered warship.

Late 1800s The repeating rifle was invented.

Early 1900's The first modern battleships were constructed in Great Britain.

1914 Airplanes were first used for reconnaissance and in battles.

1916 The British used the first modern tanks in battles against the German army.

1938 The atom was split successfully for the first time.

1939 Great Britain installed radar stations up and down its coast.

1942 The first jet aircraft was built for the U.S. Army.

1945 Atomic bombs were dropped on Hiroshima and Nagasaki.

2001 UAV's were used for U.S. military strikes in Afghanistan.

▶ Glossary

aerial warfare warfare that involves the use of flying vehicles to carry out missions and launch weapons against enemy targets.

aircraft carrier a warship designed as a base for aircraft, with a large, flat deck on which to land or take off.

airship a balloon that can be steered. An airship is filled with a gas that is lighter than air and is driven by a propeller.

ammunition bullets, shells, gunpowder, shot, and bombs that can be exploded or fired from guns or other weapons.

archer a person who shoots with bow and arrows.

armor a covering, usually of metal or leather, worn to protect the body in fighting.

artillery any gun-styled weapon that fires ammunition that is larger than bullets fired by rifles or machine guns.

atom the smallest particle of a chemical element that can take part in a chemical reaction without being permanently changed.

atomic bomb a nuclear weapon that results in an explosion of tremendous force and heat, accompanied by a blinding light.

barrel the metal tube of a gun, through which a bullet is fired.

battleship a very large warship having heavy armor and the most powerful guns.

bomber an airplane used to drop bombs on the enemy.

cannon a big gun that is too large to be carried by hand and is fixed to the ground, or mounted on a carriage or in a tank or other vehicle, or on an airplane.

carbon a very common chemical element that occurs in combination with other elements in all plants and animals.

catapult a weapon used in ancient times for shooting stones and arrows.

cavalry soldiers who fight on horseback, or a branch of the army consisting of such troops.

chariot a two-wheeled or four-wheeled vehicle, usually drawn by a horse.

chemical warfare war waged with chemicals.

chlorine a greenish-yellow, bad-smelling, poisonous gas.

civilization nations and peoples that have reached advanced stages in social development.

cold war a prolonged struggle for power between nations or groups of nations, conducted primarily by diplomatic, economic, and psychological means rather than by extensive and direct military action.

crossbow a medieval weapon for shooting arrows, consisting of a bow fixed across a wooden stock, with a groove in the middle to direct the arrows or stones.

diplomacy the management of relations between nations.

drawbridge a bridge that can be entirely or partly lifted, lowered, or moved to one side.

engineer a person who plans and builds engines, machines, roads, bridges, canals, forts, or the like.

fighter a highly maneuverable and heavily armed airplane, used mainly for attacking enemy airplanes.

fortification a wall, fort, ditch, or other defense built to make a place strong.

fortress a place built with walls and defenses.

germ a microorganism that causes disease. Germs include bacteria, viruses, and protozoa.

gunpowder a powder that goes off with noise and force when touched with fire.

grenade a small bomb, usually thrown by hand.

guided missile a missile that can be guided in flight to its target by means of radio signals from the ground or by automatic devices inside the missile that direct its course.

javelin a light spear thrown by hand.

laser a device that produces an intense, focused beam of light.

lever a bar that rests on a fixed support called a fulcrum. One end of the bar transmits force and motion to the other end, much like the action of a seesaw.

longbow a large bow, pulled back by hand, used for shooting a long, feathered arrow.

matchlock a gunlock on an old form of gun fired by lighting the charge of powder with a wick or cord.

Middle Ages the period in European history between ancient and modern times, from about the A.D. 400's through the 1400's.

musket a gun introduced in the 1500's and widely used before the development of the rifle.

Muslim relating to Islam, the name given to the religion preached by the Prophet Muhammad in the A.D. 600's.

naval; navy of the navy; all the ships of war of a country, with their officers and men and the department that manages them.

nomadic wandering; roving.

nuclear weapon a bomb, shell, rocket, guided missile, or other weapon utilizing nuclear fission or fusion as its destructive force.

radar an instrument for determining the distance, direction, and speed of unseen objects by the reflection of radio waves.

radio wave an electromagnetic wave within the radio frequencies.

rifle a gun with spiral grooves in its long barrel which spin or twist the bullet as it is shot.

rocket a device consisting of a tube open at one end and filled with some substance that burns very rapidly as fuel.

Roman of or having to do with ancient Rome or its people. The Roman Empire controlled most of Europe and the Middle East from 27 B.C. to A.D. 476.

satellite a manufactured object that continuously orbits Earth or some other body in space.

shrapnel an artillery shell filled with pellets and powder, set to explode in the air and scatter pellets or shell fragments over a wide area.

sewage water that contains waste matter produced by human beings.

steam engine an engine that is operated by the energy of expanding steam.

submarine a boat that can go underwater.

tank a heavily armored combat vehicle.

treaty an agreement, such as one between nations, that each party signs.

trench a long, narrow ditch with earth, sandbags, logs, or other shield put up in front to protect soldiers against enemy fire and attack.

turret a low, armored structure that revolves and that has guns mounted to it.

United Nations an international organization that works for world peace and human prosperity.

unmanned aerial vehicle a type of aircraft designed to fly missions without a pilot on board.

Western Front an area of contested land where many battles were fought between Germany and the Allies during World War I.

▶ Additional Resources

Books:

- *Amazing Leonardo da Vinci Inventions You Can Build Yourself* by Maxine Anderson (Nomad Press, 2006).

- *Gunpowder and Weaponry* by James Lincoln Collier (Benchmark Books, 2004).

- *Great Inventions : The Illustrated Science Encyclopedia* by Peter Harrison, Chris Oxlade, and Stephen Bennington (Southwater Publishing, 2001).

- *Great Inventions of the 20th Century* by Peter Jedicke (Chelsea House Publications, 2007).

- *Warfare in a High-Tech Age* by Sally and Adrian Morgan (Heinemann Library, 2006).

- *Weapon: A Visual History of Arms and Armor* (DK Publishing, 2006).

- *What a Great Idea! Inventions that Changed the World* by Stephen M. Tomecek (Scholastic, 2003).

Web Sites:

- The American Experience: Vietnam
  http://www.pbs.org/wgbh/amex/vietnam
  The American Experience presents an exhaustive look at the Vietnam War, including information on the people, the places, the issues, and the outcomes.

- Frontline: The Gulf War
  http://www.pbs.org/wgbh/pages/frontline/gulf/index.html
  This companion Web site to the U.S. Public Broadcasting Service television series features transcripts of interviews with key players in the war and war stories of pilots and soldiers.

- Future Weapons: Discovery Channel
  http://dsc.discovery.com/tv/future-weapons/future-weapons.html
  A companion site to Discovery Channel's Future Weapons television series.

- NASA'S History of Rockets
  http://www.grc.nasa.gov/WWW/K-12/TRC/Rockets/history_of_rockets.html
  A history of rockets and aeronautics from the U.S. National Aeronautics and Space Administration.

- National Inventors Hall of Fame
  http://www.invent.org/index.asp
  Information on inventions and inventors from the U.S. National Inventors Hall of Fame.

- Top 10 Weapons in History
  http://www.space.com/technology/top10_weapons_history.html
  Includes information about the most important weapons in history.

- Weapons Through Time (BBC)
  http://www.bbc.co.uk/history/british/launch_gms_weapons_thru_time.shtml
  A game that tests your knowledge of what weapons were used during conflicts throughout history. Includes links to information about world wars and warriors throughout history.

▶ Index

A
aerial warfare, 32-33, 36-39
Agent Orange, 29
airplane, 32-33, 38-39
airship, 36-37
Alcázar (Spain), 12
Alexander the Great, 8
American Revolution, 27, 32
armor, body, 7, 16-17, 22
artillery, 14, 24-25, 29
atomic bomb, 40-41

B
balloon. *See* airship
battery, 24
battleship, 32-33
Big Bertha, 25
biological warfare, 28-29
bomber, 38-39
bow and arrow, 6-7, 16
bulletproof vest, 17

C
cannon, 15, 18, 24-25; hand, 20-21
castle, 12-13
catapult, 14-15
cavalry, 8-9
chain mail, 16
chariot, 9
chemical warfare, 28-29
China, 18, 22, 26, 28, 36
claymore, 10
Comprehensive Nuclear Test Ban
    Treaty, 41
Congreve, William, 26
crossbow, 7, 16

D
drawbridge, 13
Dreadnought (ship), 32

E
Egypt, ancient, 4, 5, 6, 8
Einstein, Albert, 41

F
fighter, 38-39
firearm, 11, 17. *See also* artillery; gun;
    gunpowder
flak jacket, 17
fort and fortress, 12-14, 24, 25
Fulton, Robert, 31

G
Gatling, Richard, 23
Gatling gun, 23
Germany, 25-29, 35, 37, 39
Giffard, Henri, 36
gladiator, 17
Greece, ancient, 7, 14, 16, 28, 30
gun, 20-23
gunpowder, 11, 15, 18-20, 30

H
harquebus, 20, 21
Harry S. Truman (ship), 33
Hiroshima (Japan), 40, 41
Hittites, 8
horse, 8-9, 17
howitzer, 25

I
invention, 4

J
Japan, 10-11, 33, 40, 41
javelin, 6

L
Lana, Francesco de, 36
laser, 43

M
machine gun, 23
Macon (airship), 37
Manhattan Project, 41
matchlock, 20-21
Maxim, Hiram, 23
Megiddo, Battle of, 5
Middle Ages, 7, 9-11, 16, 28
missile, 26-27
moat, 13
mortar, 24-25
musket, 22

N
Nagasaki (Japan), 40, 41
Napoléon Bonaparte, 24, 26
Non-Proliferation of Nuclear Weapons,
    Treaty on, 41
nuclear weapon, 40-41

O
Oppenheimer, J. Robert, 41

P
Pearl Harbor (Hawaii), 33
Persia, ancient, 6, 10

R
rapier, 10
Raptor (jet), 39
Red Baron, 39
repeating rifle, 23
revolver, 21
Richthofen, Manfred von, 39
rifle, 18, 22-23
rocket, 26-27
Rome, ancient, 14, 16, 17, 30

S
samurai, 10-11
scimitar, 10
ship, 30-33
shotgun, 21
Soviet Union, 9, 27
Spanish Armada, 30-31
spear, 6-7
steam engine, 31, 36
submarine, 32
sword, 10-11

T
tank, 34-35
Thutmose III, 5
trench warfare, 25, 34

U
United Nations, 41
unmanned aerial vehicle (UAV), 42-43

V
V-1 and V-2 rockets, 27
Vietnam War, 29
Vikings, 30

W
warfare, 4-5
warship, 30-33
World War I, 9, 15, 17, 32; aerial war-
    fare, 36-39; artillery, 25; chemical
    warfare, 28-29; machine guns, 23;
    tanks, 34-35
World War II: airplanes, 38-39; atomic
    bomb, 40-41; cavalry, 9; rockets,
    26-27; tanks, 34-35; warships, 32,
    33

Z
zeppelin, 36-37
Zeppelin, Ferdinand von, 36